Welcome to South Korea

By Patrick Ryan

The Child's World®

Published by The Child's World®
1980 Lookout Drive
Mankato, MN 56003-1705
800-599-READ
www.childsworld.com

Content Adviser: Hongkyung Kim, Ph.D., Assistant Professor,
Program in Korean Studies, Department of Asian & Asian American Studies,
State University of New York at Stony Brook, Stony Brook, NY
Design and Production: The Creative Spark, San Juan Capistrano, CA
Editorial: Publisher's Diner, Wendy Mead, Greenwich, CT
Photo Research: Deborah Goodsite, Califon, NJ

Cover and title page photo: PCL/Alamy
Interior photos: Alamy: 8 (Pieder), 18 (Trip), 22 (JTB Photo Communications, Inc.); Animals
Animals/Earth Scenes: 19 (Manfred Gottschalk); Corbis: 10 (Michel Setboun), 3 bottom, 16, 27
(Cha Young-Jin/epa), 17 (Atlantide Phototravel), 21 (Catherine Karnow), 23 (Nathan Benn); Getty
Images: 25 (Chung Sung-Jun); iStockphoto.com: 7 bottom (Sebastian Schäfer), 28 top (P. Wel), 28
bottom (David Franklin), 31 (Iwan Drago); Landov: 12 (REUTERS/Kim Kyung-Hoon); NASA Earth
Observatory: 4 (Reto Stockli); Panos Pictures: 24 (Chris Stowers), 30 (Mark Henley); Peter Arnold,
Inc.: 3 middle, 9 (Wolfgang Poelzer), 20 (Jean-Léo Dugast); Photolibrary Group: 3 top, 6, 11, 13, 14;
SuperStock: 7 top (age fotostock), 15 (Steve Vidler).

Library of Congress Cataloging-in-Publication Data
Ryan, Patrick, 1948–
  Welcome to South Korea / by Patrick Ryan.
       p. cm. — (Welcome to the world)
  Includes index.
  ISBN 978-1-59296-978-4 (library bound : alk. paper)
  1. Korea (South)—Juvenile literature. I. Title. II. Series.

DS902.R98 2008
951.95—dc22

                                              2007036354

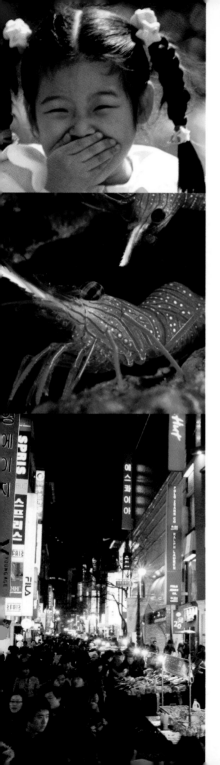

Contents

Where Is South Korea? 4

The Land 6

Plants and Animals 8

Long Ago 10

South Korea Today 12

The People 15

City Life and Country Life 16

Schools and Language 18

Work 21

Food 22

Pastimes 25

Holidays 26

Fast Facts About South Korea 28

How Do You Say... 30

Glossary 31

Further Information 32

Index 32

Where Is South Korea?

Earth is a big place. It has huge oceans and frozen areas known as ice caps. It also has large land areas called **continents.** Some continents are made up of many different countries. South Korea is a country on the continent of Asia. South Korea is part of a land area called a **peninsula.** A peninsula has water almost all of the way around it. South Korea shares its peninsula with the country of North Korea.

This picture gives us a flat look at Earth. South Korea is inside the red circle.

Did you **know?**

South Korea is really called the "Republic of Korea." People just say "South Korea" for short.

NORTH
KOREA

A   S   I   A

Demilitarized Zone

Seoraksan ▲

SOUTH KOREA

⭐ National capital
● Other city

East Sea

⭐ Seoul

● Incheon

Taebaek Mountains

Yellow Sea

● Andong

● Daejeon

● Daegu

● Chunghak-dong

● Gwangju

● Busan

Korea Strait

0   30   60 miles
0   30   60 kilometers

N
W ⊗ E
S

Tsushima Strait

JAPAN

Jeju ●
▲ *Hallasan*

Jeju-do

The Land

South Korea has many rocky mountains and hills. Besides the mountains, South Korea also has a few forests and flat plains. Some mountain areas and plains are used for farming.

Seoraksan is a mountain that can be found in the northeast part of the country.

There are rivers that flow through the countryside, too. Many islands can be found near South Korea's coasts. Islands are land areas that are surrounded by water on all sides.

Many people visit the island of Jeju-do to enjoy its natural beauty.

Did you **know?**

The highest point in South Korea is Hallasan, which stands 6,398 feet (1,950 meters) above sea level on Jeju-do.

Plants and Animals

A pine tree near Busan

The lands of South Korea are full of life. Many different types of trees grow there, including pine trees, chestnut trees, oak trees, and gingko trees. Maple and elm trees can also be found there, too. The thick woods hide many shy animals, such as deer and mice. Bears, wild pigs, and many kinds of birds also live there. And the deep ocean waters near South Korea's shore are home to all kinds of fish and other water creatures.

These shrimp are just a few of the animals that live in South Korea's waters.

Long Ago

Long ago, Korea was made up of many small kingdoms. Over time, the little kingdoms joined together. They formed three large kingdoms called Goguryeo, Baekje, and Silla. These kingdoms battled for control until the Silla kingdom united them in 668. They ruled Korea until 918.

The ruins of an ancient temple in Chunghak-dong

After the Silla, other **dynasties** followed. The last dynasty, known as the Joseon dynasty, lasted more than five hundred years. During this time, people had many beliefs that are still important to Koreans today, such as working hard and caring for their elders.

In 1910, however, Korea's quiet ways were shattered when the country was taken over by Japan. Japan later fought in World War II and was defeated. When the war was over, Korea was split into two countries. North Korea and South Korea were given their own names and their own governments. But both sides were unhappy. They both wanted to control all of Korea.

This statue stands at Deoksugung, a palace used by Korean rulers for hundreds of years.

11

South Korea Today

As the two Koreas tried to reunite their lands, fighting began. People from the north began attacking people from the south. This conflict was called the Korean War. After three years of fighting, both sides agreed to stop.

Did you know?

The area that separates North and South Korea is called the Demilitarized (deh-MIL-ih-teh-ryzd) Zone (DMZ). It was set up at the end of the Korean War to keep the two fighting countries apart. The DMZ is more than 2 miles (3.2 kilometers) wide and 150 miles (241.4 kilometers) long.

A worker checks DVD players at a factory.

Since the war, South Korea has become a strong and successful nation. People from all around the world can buy cars, computers, and other electronics made there. It also has a large army.

13

Less than one-fourth of South Korea's population is under the age of fourteen.

The People

About 49 million people live in South Korea. Most of them are Koreans who were born there. Their ancestors were members of different **Mongol** tribes that came to the area from Central Asia. Over the years, many **immigrants,** or newcomers from other countries, have been coming to South Korea, too. They are looking for good jobs and places to live. Most of South Korea's immigrants come from South Asia.

These women are wearing traditional Korean clothing.

City Life and Country Life

Shoppers visit stores at night in the country's capital city, Seoul.

Most South Koreans live in cities. They live in apartments or small houses and work in offices, stores, and factories. South Korean cities have fast cars, crowded streets, and subway systems just like those in the United States. Some South Korean cities are very large, too. Seoul, the capital city, has more than 10 million people.

Did you know?

About two hundred years ago, Seoul was a walled city with gates that closed at night.

Two women take a walk through the village of Andong.

South Korea's country people live differently. Instead of
tall apartment buildings, they live in simple houses made
from wood and bricks. They work on the land or the sea,
farming or fishing until the sun goes down. Some country
people also travel to the cities to work.

17

Students work on an assignment in class.

Schools and Language

South Korean children start school at an early age. They often attend preschools before they go to kindergarten. In elementary school, they learn reading and writing just as you do. They also learn math. The alphabet in South Korea is called *hangeul*. It has 24 letters. South Koreans use a few Chinese symbols when they write, too.

The official language of South Korea is Korean. Unlike other languages, it borrows many words from the Chinese language. There are also several **dialects,** or forms, of the language spoken in different areas of the country.

A school group visits a palace in Seoul.

Fishing boats crowd the harbor in Busan.

Work

On the island of Jeju-do, workers harvest potatoes, one of the many crops grown in South Korea.

Many of the products we use come from South Korea. Cars, televisions, running shoes, and clothing are just a few of the things made there. Parts for computers and cellular phones also come from South Korean factories. South Korea's rich farmland grows beans, potatoes, barley, and different kinds of vegetables for the nation's people. Many people work long hours to catch fish with huge nets. Whatever their job is, most South Koreans work very hard.

Food

Rice is the most important food in South Korea. It is eaten at almost every meal. Fish, barley, peaches, beans, and sweet

A bowl of *kimchi*

potatoes are important foods, too. South Koreans also like spices. One popular dish, called *kimchi* (KIM-chee), is made with cabbage, radishes, garlic, and red peppers. People make it in many different ways. Sometimes kimchi is very spicy.

A Korean family enjoys a meal together in Seoul.

These children attend a martial arts class in Jeju.

Pastimes

South Koreans love to have fun. They like such sports as soccer, basketball, baseball, and tennis. They also like to go to concerts, plays, and movies, just as you do. Other popular pastimes include **martial arts.** Martial arts teach people how to defend themselves. Tae kwon do (TEY KWAN DOH) is a popular martial art in South Korea.

A child takes his sled for a ride down a hill.

25

Holidays

South Koreans celebrate many holidays and hold lots of festivals. In late January or early February they celebrate their **Lunar** New Year. People dress in their best clothes and remember their relatives of long ago. Then it is time to enjoy a big feast.

South Koreans also have fun family celebrations. Weddings and birthdays are very happy times. They are celebrated with special foods and gifts. Family members all gather to talk and laugh together on these days.

South Korea is a small country that is growing stronger every day. After many difficult years, South Koreans are working hard to keep their country safe and successful. Perhaps one day you will visit this beautiful land of hills and mountains. If you do, look around—and remember to enjoy its rocky terrain, green forests, and attractive coastlines.

Wearing traditional costumes, these dancers are performing at a New Year's celebration.

Area: About 38,000 square miles (98,420 square kilometers)—a little larger than Indiana.

Population: About 49 million people

Capitol City: Seoul

Other Important Cities: Busan, Daegu, Incheon, Gwangju, Daejeon

Money: The won

National Holidays: South Korea has many national holidays including Memorial Day on June 6 and Liberation Day on August 15.

National Language: Korean

National Flag: White with black bars and a circle of red and blue in the middle. The white stands for purity. The red and blue stand for cooperation and togetherness. The black bars stand for things such as the four seasons and the four directions.

Chief of State: President

Head of Government: Prime minister

Famous South Koreans:

Kim Dae Jung: former president and Nobel Peace Prize winner

Ban Ki-moon: politician and secretary-general of the United Nations

Ku Sang: writer

Chung Ju Young: businessman, founder of Hyundai Group

National Song: *"Aegukga"* (Patriotic Song)

Until the East Sea's waves are dry,
Baek-du-san worn away,
God watch o'er our land forever!
Our Korea hail!

[chorus] Rose of Sharon, thousand miles of
beautiful mountain and rivers!
Guarded by her people, ever may Korea stand!

Like that South Mountain armored
Pine, standing on duty still,
Wind or frost, unchanging ever, be our
   resolute will.

[chorus]

In autumn's arching evening sky,
Crystal, and cloudless blue,
Be the radiant moon our spirit,
Steadfast, single and true.

[chorus]

With such a will, such a spirit, loyalty,
   heart and hand,
Let us love, come grief, come gladness,
   this, our beloved land!

[chorus]

South Korean Recipe*: **Vegetable Pancakes**

These tasty pancakes can be made with shrimp or other seafood. You can add some of your favorite vegetables—finely chopped—to the mix, too.

2 cups flour
2 eggs
2 cups water
A bunch of scallions
½ cup grated carrot

½ teaspoon salt
oil
6 tablespoons soy sauce
2 tablespoons rice or white vinegar
2 teaspoons sugar

Mix flour, eggs, and water together in a large bowl. Have an adult help you chop the scallions (use only the green parts) and grate the carrot. Then add the vegetables along with the salt to the batter. Coat the bottom of a fry pan with oil and heat up pan on the stove. Add ½ cup of batter into the hot pan. Cook for two to three minutes until browned. Then flip pancake over and cook the second side for another two minutes. Continue to make pancakes until you have used up all of the batter. Cut the pancakes into wedge-shaped pieces. Mix soy sauce, vinegar, and sugar together and use as a sauce for the pancakes.

Always ask an adult for permission and help when using the kitchen.

29

How Do You Say...

ENGLISH	KOREAN	HOW TO SAY IT
Hello	annyong haseyo	ahn-yong hay-sey-yoh
Goodbye	annyong	ahn-yong
Please	putakhamnida	poo-tak-hahm-nee-dah
Thank You	kamsahamnida	kahm-sah-hahm-nee-dah
One	hana	hah-nah
Two	tul	tool
Three	set	sett
South Korea	Nam Ham	nam hahm

Glossary

continents (KON-tih-nents) Earth's huge land areas are called continents. South Korea is on the continent of Asia.

dialects (DY-uh-lekts) Dialects are local variations of a spoken language. Like English, Korean has many different dialects.

dynasties (DY-nuh-steez) Dynasties are families of rulers. Many of Korea's rulers came from dynasties.

immigrants (IM-ih-grents) Immigrants are newcomers from other countries. Many South Koreans are immigrants from China.

lunar (LOO-nar) Lunar means having to do with the moon. A lunar calendar, one based on the movements of the moon, is used to figure out when to celebrate Lunar New Year.

martial arts (MAR-shull ARTS) Martial arts are activities that teach people how to defend themselves. Many South Koreans practice martial arts.

Mongol (MON-gul) A mongol is a member of one of the roaming tribes in Mongolia. People from some of those groups came to South Korea long ago.

peninsula (puh-NIN-soo-luh) A peninsula is a land area that has water most of the way around it. South Korea lies on a peninsula that is attached to the continent of Asia.

Further Information

Read It

Bowden, Rob. *South Korea.* New York: Facts on File, 2006.

Kwek, Karen, Johanna Masse, Melvin Neo, and Dorothy L. Gibbs. *Welcome to South Korea.* Milwaukee, WI: Gareth Stevens, 2003.

McMahon, Patricia, and Michael F. O'Brien. *Chi-Hoon: A Korean Girl.* Honesdale, PA: Boyds Mills Press, 1998.

Look It Up

Visit our Web page for lots of links about South Korea:
http://www.childsworld.com/links

Note to Parents, Teachers, and Librarians: We routinely verify our Web links to make sure they are safe, active sites—so encourage your readers to check them out!

32

Index

animals, 8
area, 28
capital city, 16, 28
education, 18
farming, 6, 21
flag, 28
food, 22
government, 11, 12, 28
Hallasan (mountain), 7
history, 10–11, 12
holidays, 26
industries, 13, 21
Jeju-do, 7
Korean War, 12
language, 18–19
major cities, 28
money, 28
national song, 29
natural resources, 6, 21
plants, 8
population, 15
sports, 25